BREAK THE CYCLE

ISBN: 978-1-63950-108-3   [Paperback Edition]
            978-1-63950-110-6   [Hardback Edition]
            978-1-63950-109-0   [eBook Edition]

Originally published 2020 by Xlibris.

Printed and bound in The United States of America.
Certain stock photos © Shutterstock.com.

Writers Apex

Gateway Towards Success

+13176596889
www.writersapex.com
8063 MADISON AVE #1252
Indianapolis, IN 46227

BREAK THE CYCLE

I WAS THE MISTRESS BEFORE
I WAS THE WIFE; NOW I'M THE EX-WIFE, TOO

Ros B

CONTENTS

DEDICATION

This book is dedicated to all who are brokenhearted.

"He healeth the broken in heart, and bindeth
up their wounds" (Psa. 147:3).

"Blessed be God, even the Father of our Lord Jesus Christ,
the Father of mercies, and the God of all comfort; Who
comforteth us in all our tribulation, that we may be able
to comfort them which are in any trouble, by the comfort
wherewith we ourselves are comforted of God" (2 Cor. 1:3–4).

ACKNOWLEDGEMENTS

First and foremost, I thank God, for in Him I live and move and have my being. Without Him, I can do nothing. I thank Him for bringing me through the most painful and difficult time of my life. He never left me nor forsook me. To God be the glory for the things He has done!

I thank my family for loving and supporting me and for giving me the space I needed to go through the healing process. Thank you for allowing me to stay in my cocoon until God finished changing me into a beautiful butterfly. Thank you for allowing me to stay buried until I could break through and blossom.

To my Augusta and Rock Hill families, I still love you back.

Thank you to my coworkers LaTanya, Milet, Patty, and Valerie for my surprise birthday gift.

Thank you to all of you who crossed my path, whether for good or for bad. "And we know that all things work together for good to them that love God, to them who are the called according to his purpose" (Rom. 8:28). Without you all, I would not be who I am today. May God continue to strengthen you, keep you, and bless you.

"This is the Lord's doing; it is marvellous in our eyes"
(Psa. 118:23)

CHAPTER 1

Lord, Please Send Me a Friend

After I left the military, I was lonely for companionship. None of my previous attempts at relationships had been successful, so I decided to turn to God. I prayed, *Lord, please send me a friend. I want somebody to do things with, to go places with. Someone to love me. Someone I can love.*

It was midnight when I walked into Club Sapphire. The music met me at the door and led me to the ballroom. I stood against the wall and checked the place out, wanting to give myself time to adjust to the dim lighting and the massive sea of Friday night clubgoers. My period of adjustment didn't last long, though. As soon as the guys realized there was a new face in the room, they started to swarm like a hive of bees in my direction. Some guy came up to me and asked me to dance. I refused. Another guy asked me to dance. When I refused him, he told me I must be gay. After a few more unwanted advances,

I made my way to the bar. *Maybe a change of location would give me some relief,* I thought.

"Coke, please," I told the bartender.

I was alone and driving, so I had to pass on the alcohol.

As the bartender placed my drink in front of me, I heard a male voice behind me.

"I see we're drinking the same thing," he said in a smooth baritone voice. He was just over six feet tall, and I knew I would fit perfectly under his arm. He had short, wavy, black hair and deep dimples that I instantly fell in love with. He flashed me a gorgeous, wide smile with all pearly whites, and I immediately felt comfortable with him. His light-brown eyes gazed into mine, drawing me in. He wore a soft, musky cologne that made me want to breathe in more deeply. He was very handsome, and I was not going to pass on this one.

"Oh, you're drinking Coke, too?" I asked, giving him a warm smile.

"Yes, I'm the designated driver tonight. Me and the guys hang out every weekend. Sometimes we check out a club or two. And tonight, we are celebrating my new job!

"I have a table over there. You want to join me?" he asked, pointing to a table across the room.

Why not? I prayed for a friend. And I certainly won't find one sitting alone at the bar.

"Sure," I responded. "That sounds nice."

"I'm Kevin."

"Hi, Kevin. I'm Kay, short for Kayleigh."

We moved to his table, and he introduced me to his friends

Jake, Larry, and Marcos, whom he had bonded with in the military. After a few moments, they all discreetly disappeared and left Kevin and me alone. I was surprised by how easily the conversation flowed between us. We talked for what seemed like hours, and I learned quite a bit about him. On Monday, he was starting his new job as the laboratory supervisor in the emergency department at City Medical Center. He had just retired from the military after twenty years of service. He had been born and raised here in Pedro, California. He had two older brothers and three younger sisters.

Kevin told me he was divorced and had two daughters. He had been married for nine years, and things just hadn't worked out. He and his wife had grown apart and were more like roommates than husband and wife. She did her thing, and he did his.

He shared some details of his military career with me. He'd had a lot of assignments overseas, including Germany, Spain, and Korea. All of them were exciting, and he'd had a ball at each one. He kept me laughing about the antics of him and his comrades. *Wow! Kevin is amazing. I'm glad I decided to give him a chance.*

As our conversation flowed, I found myself sharing just as much about me. I normally didn't divulge so many personal details when first meeting a guy. It usually took months for me to open up this much. But there was just something about Kevin that put me at ease.

"I'm not married—no children."

I went on to tell him I had just separated from the military after six years of service and had moved to Pedro from my hometown in South Carolina. I had been raised in a small town. Now I wanted something different. The West Coast was definitely different! I also worked at City Medical Center, in the chemistry department in the main lab. I had been there for eight years.

I was the youngest of twelve children, four boys and eight girls. My mom and most of my family still lived in and around my hometown. I had traveled to Turkey and Japan. When he talked about his assignment in Germany, I told him that when I was stationed at Incirlik, Turkey, I had visited Germany. And I told him about how much I loved the Autobahn. Amazing! And while I was stationed at Misawa, Japan, I had visited Hawaii, a very beautiful, although very expensive, place. I loved the random rain showers during the day and the luaus at night. It was the perfect honeymoon spot.

Around three in the morning, they closed the dance floor. Neither one of us was ready to leave, so Kevin called a cab for his buddies.

"Oh, you just gon' kick us to the curb, huh?" Jake ribbed him.

"You know how it is, man," Kevin said flashing that gorgeous smile again. "I'll catch y'all later."

And he and I moved to a smaller ballroom, where jazz was playing. Kevin said he loved jazz and named some of his favorite artists.

"What are you doing later today?" he asked.

"I don't have any plans." I responded, hoping he'd ask me out. And he did!

"Would you like to go out with me?"

I paused. I didn't want him to know how excited I was.

"Sure. I'd like that," I said, smiling brightly.

Around four in the morning, they closed the club. As Kevin walked me to my car, he asked for my phone number. I gave it to him, and we talked some more. Finally, everyone started leaving, so we reluctantly said our goodbyes.

On our first date, Kevin and I went bowling in Quentin, about fifty miles up the coast. He didn't hold back at all. He bowled strike after strike, and he beat me badly. I could see he was very competitive. Well, I was a sore loser, so I pouted. He hugged me, kissed me on the cheek, and apologized for beating me. "I play to win," he whispered in my ear as he pulled me close.

Next, we went to the movies. I would have chosen drama, but he chose action. It turned out to be a very good movie. We both enjoyed it. We ordered hot dogs, chips, candy, and drinks. After the movie, we weren't ready to part company, so he asked if he could come over to my place. I reluctantly agreed. He was still a stranger to me, and I wanted to be careful. But I wasn't ready for the night to end either, so I told him he could come to my place.

We sat on the couch in the living room, and we talked some more. I flipped through the TV channels, trying to find something interesting to watch on a Saturday night. I stopped on a movie that looked appealing. In the movie, this couple were arguing in the bedroom. After a while, the man gently grabbed the woman by her upper arms and started kissing her as he laid her back on the bed.

Kevin said to me, "I want to do that."

I smiled and continued flipping channels.

"Can I get you something to drink?" I asked.

"No, but you can kiss me."

Kevin moved closer to me on the couch and leaned toward me. I ignored him and kept my eyes on the television.

"Can I kiss you?"

I didn't answer, so he leaned in closer.

"Is that a yes?" he asked.

He cupped my chin and gently touched my lips with his.

I can't do this, I thought. *I don't even know him. What will he think of me?*

I pulled away, and he stopped. After a while, he said, "I'd better go. Thank you for a wonderful evening. Can I see you tomorrow?"

"Yes," I responded.

"Okay. When is a good time to call you?"

"Anytime is fine," I answered.

On Sunday, Kevin and I went to the best seafood restaurant in Quentin for dinner. We both ordered the seafood platter. We had easy conversation. I studied him as he talked. He seemed like such a nice guy. He had nice thin, kissable lips, a neatly trimmed mustache, and gorgeous dimples in each cheek. I'm a sucker for dimples. Kevin also had short, wavy black hair. Mmm. Sexy. He was dark-skinned and just over six feet tall.

Yes, tall, dark, and handsome! As I looked at Kevin across the table, I thought, *Could this be my knight in shining armor?*

After dinner, Kevin came back to my place. Earlier that day, I had bought some Najee, Kenny G., Gerald Albright, Grover Washington, David Sanborn, Kirk Whalum, Fourplay, and Spyro Gyra music. We listened to jazz and talked. After a while, he moved closer to me on the couch and looked into my eyes. I was mesmerized.

"You are so beautiful," he said.

Kevin leaned in and brushed my lips with his. He looked at me again and pulled me into his arms. He started kissing me gently at first, and then urgently. I didn't resist this time. I gave into the passion building between us. I felt a strong connection to him, and I wanted more. That night, we became one in the flesh.

Monday, I met Shannon for lunch. She and I had had orientation together when we started working at City Medical Center and had become close friends over the years. She was a registered nurse in the emergency department. "Girl, what happened to you? I didn't hear from you all weekend." Oops. She had texted me, but I had forgotten to respond.

"I was a little preoccupied."

"Who is it this time?"

I smiled. "The new lab supervisor."

"You go, girl! I wasn't here when he interviewed. But I heard he was fine. He was all they talked about for a while."

"That—he is."

Kevin kept in touch all week. I did not see him at work, but he kept me updated on his transition. He came to my place Wednesday for a couple of hours and again on Friday, but he did not spend the night. I wondered about that but did not say anything.

I didn't hear anything from Kevin all the next week. I called him a couple of times and got no answer. I left a message but got no return call. I was disappointed, but I continued my week, as usual.

Friday morning, Kevin called. He said he would be busy this weekend and couldn't see me. He said he'd call when he could, but he had a lot going on.

Really? I thought sarcastically.

For the next two months, Kevin and I sort of dated. I think it was more about sex than anything. He called me when he wanted me, but I could never reach him. He would come over on Friday or Saturday, and we would do something together. Most Fridays, we stayed in and watched movies. If he couldn't make it on Friday, he would come on Saturday. Most Saturdays, we would go out to dinner and either bowling, skating, or to the park, and always in Quentin or Mesa, about fifty miles east of Pedro. Kevin said there were more options in Quentin and Mesa, and he loved to drive. I loved the walks in the park, nature, fresh air, and the closeness and intimacy we shared.

Kevin always came to my house; he never invited me to his, and we always had sex.

One Friday, Kevin came over and brought a single red rose.

"I'm falling in love with you," he said.

We watched a movie on television, and then we made passionate love. Afterward, I lay in his arms in bed and thought about how wonderful he was, how good he made me feel.

"I love you, babe," he said.

I thought I was starting to fall in love with him, too. But it felt as if it was too soon for me to say it back.

Kevin went to the bathroom to freshen up. I heard his phone ringing in his pants pocket. I was on such a high that I took it out to answer it. *He's my man; I'm sure I can answer his phone. He won't mind. Will he?*

"When were you going to tell me you were married?" I asked calmly as Kevin came out of the bathroom.

"Huh?" he asked innocently.

"You heard me! Your wife just called!" I yelled, holding up his cell phone.

"Babe ..." he started.

"Get out!" I screamed as I threw his phone at him, aiming for his head. He ducked.

"Babe, let me explain," he said as he picked up his phone off the floor.

"I said get out," I repeated as coldly as I could.

He walked toward me, reaching out his arms. "Babe, you don't understand. We're separated. We're divorcing."

"You said you *were* divorced."

"I'm sorry. I didn't mean to lie to you. I just wanted to get to know you."

"Kevin, get your lying behind out of my house, now!" I yelled.

He threw his hands up and sighed. He looked at me. I stared at him. He grabbed his clothes and walked out of my bedroom. A few minutes later, I heard the front door close. I sat on the side of the bed, put my head in my hands, and cried. I couldn't believe this.

The man I was falling in love with was married.

The man I was falling in love with had lied to me.

The man I was falling for was somebody else's man.

CHAPTER 2

Oh Lord, What Have I Done?

The next week, Kevin called and texted me every day throughout the day, leaving messages that he was sorry for misleading me. He loved me. He and his wife were separated and were getting divorced. He even waited for me at my car one day after work. I told him to stay away from me and that I would file a complaint if he continued to bother me. Finally, he stopped harassing me.

Three months later, I came home from work, and Kevin was waiting outside my house with a dozen roses.

"Can we talk, please?" he pleaded.

"There's nothing to talk about," I said, brushing past him.

"Kay, I'm divorced," he said, holding up divorce papers.

The divorce had been finalized on Wednesday. Today was Friday.

I wasn't looking forward to another lonely weekend. He had

a dozen roses. He looked good. He smelled good. *What the heck,* I thought, and I let him in.

Kevin waited in the living room while I changed my clothes and got comfortable.

What am I doing? I kept asking myself. *He lied to me. How can I ever trust him?*

But he said he just wanted to get to know me. He didn't plan on falling in love.

"We need to talk," I said as I entered the living room.

Kevin was relaxing on the couch. "What's up, babe?" he asked.

"How long were you married?" I asked.

"Nine years."

"What happened?"

"We had different ideas of marriage, and we grew apart. She wanted the house on the hill with maid service. She hated to cook and clean, and she shopped all the time. There was no room in the closet for my clothes, eventually. She even took over the guest room. I had to close out our joint checking account because we were always in the negative, always paying insufficient funds fees. She didn't talk to me about major purchases; she just purchased."

"Didn't you know that before you married her?"

"Yeah, but I thought she would change."

"Did she agree to the divorce, or did you just file?"

"She didn't care one way or the other. She was doing her own thing."

"How can I be sure you won't do the same thing to me five years from now?"

"Baby, I would never cheat on you. I love you."

"Didn't you love her?"

"Honestly—no."

"Then why did you marry her?"

"Seemed like a good idea at the time."

Kevin came over often after that, and I was always able to get in touch with him. He was so kind and thoughtful.

One Sunday evening, Marcos, one of Kevin's military buddies, and his wife Rachel invited us out to dinner. Jake and his wife Gina and Larry and his wife Sara joined us. Jake and Gina were seasoned citizens, and they seemed like nice people. Larry and Sara were a few years older than Kevin and me. Marcos and Rachel were our age. They all seemed like great people, and they welcomed me with open arms.

We went to Country Buffet on Gordon Highway in Pedro. There was so much food to choose from: fried chicken, baked chicken, smothered pork chops, country-fried steak, Salisbury steak, chicken livers and gizzards, collard greens, cabbage, okra and tomatoes, rice, mashed potatoes, macaroni and cheese, and all kinds of desserts: pecan pie, sweet potato pie, chocolate cake, coconut cake, strawberry shortcake, bread pudding—I felt like I was in the country again. We all ate our fill.

Jake always walked with his head in the air and a big smile on his face. His wife told him that one day he was going to walk into a wall. Gina, Sara, and Rachel were straightforward people. They didn't mind telling it like it was. Rachel was a riot. She was always saying something funny. Larry and Marcos were perfect gentlemen, very respectful to everybody. I fell in love with them all right away. They embraced me like family. Every Sunday after service, we went to dinner. Rachel was the food connoisseur. She always picked where we ate. "Rachel, where are we going today?" one of us would ask. We made the rounds to Piccadilly, Country Buffett, China Buffet, Red Lobster, Ruby Tuesday, TGIF …

Kevin asked me an odd question one day. "Will you go to church with me?"

"You go to church?" I asked incredulously. In all the time we had been together—after all the long conversations—Kevin had never once said a single word about church.

"Yes, I do!" he said indignantly. "I try to do right."

I never would have guessed.

"One of my sisters is an evangelist, and she is preaching for Women's Day. I love to hear her preach, and I support her as much as possible." He said.

I grew up in the Apostolic church. My mother dragged us to church every Sunday morning for Sunday School and morning service, and every Sunday evening, every Wednesday night for Bible study, and every Friday night for another service. Two nights a week and all day long on Sundays, we were in church. Finally, in high school, she let me stay home on Wednesdays to do homework.

My mother was very strict, and because I was the youngest, she was overprotective. I couldn't go anywhere because she was afraid something would happen to me. In high school, one of my brothers rescued me on the weekends. He took me to the games at school, and I stayed at his house afterward. Mom put the television on the back porch because it was a sin to watch. She only kept it at all to watch the news in case of an emergency. I couldn't wear pants. She cut in on my phone conversations with my boyfriends. When I left home, church was the last thing on my mind. I was finally free, free to do me. I tried the services on base, however, but they didn't do anything for me. I was used to that hand-clapping, foot-stomping, all-day service that was in my blood.

Sunday morning, I decided to wear my red-and-white flowery dress. Someone told me red was my color, and I always got compliments when I wore it. I texted Kevin that I was leaving my house, and I drove to the church. It was a beautiful dark-red brick building. Kevin was waiting for me as I pulled into the parking lot. He looked so good in a black polo shirt and black slacks. He held the door open for me as I got out of the car, and we walked into the church together. It was beautiful inside as well, with red carpet and comfortable red pews. The windows were stained glass of a mosaic design with reds, oranges, blues, and greens. This was Kevin's childhood church, and most of his family still attended.

The women's choir was already in place, and the service began. During one of the songs, the pastor and his wife walked into the sanctuary. She took her seat in the pulpit on the left side, and he proceeded to his chair in the middle of the pulpit. Behind them, the ministers followed and filled the four chairs on each side of the pastor. That choir could sing, and we had an awesome service!

Evangelist Rochelle preached about the woman at the well. Her topic, "What Are You Thirsty For?" was taken from the Gospel according to John in the King James Version.

John 4:13–14: "Jesus answered and said unto her, Whosoever drinketh of this water shall thirst again: But whosoever drinketh of the water that I shall give him shall never thirst; but the water that I shall give him shall be in him a well of water springing up into everlasting life."

John 4:17–18: "The woman answered and said, I have no husband. Jesus said unto her, Thou hast well said, I have no husband: For thou hast had five husbands; and he whom thou now hast is not thy husband: in that saidst thou truly."

Thirsty: "The feeling of needing to drink something. It occurs whenever the body is dehydrated for any reason. It occurs because of lack."[1]

"Deficient in moisture."[2]

"Having or showing a strong desire or need for something."[3]

"Eagerly desirous."[4]

"Craving something."[5]

In the text, Jesus was on his way to Galilee from Judea. Most Jews bypassed Samaria, which is on the way, and took the longer route around Samaria. They believed the Samaritans were unclean. Jesus, however, went through Samaria. He rested by a well, and a Samaritan woman went to the well to draw water.

Jesus asked her for a drink, and a conversation was started. Jesus revealed that the woman had been with six different men. This woman was thirsty for love, comfort, and security. She was lacking something, and she sought fulfillment in men. Like this Samaritan woman, many of us lack something in our lives, but instead of turning to Jesus, we seek fulfillment in everything else. However, there are costs when we try to fill the empty space with anything other than Jesus.

I. Are you thirsty for pornography and sex?

Some people turn to pornography and sex for fulfillment. Every second, over $3,000 are spent on pornography, and over 28,000 people are watching it. Every thirty-nine minutes, a new porn video is created. The porn business brings in over $13 billion in the United States and over $97 billion globally. There are over 4 million porn websites.[6]

About 38 percent of men and 45 percent of women with sex addictions have a venereal disease, and close to 70 percent of women with sex addictions said they had at least one unwanted pregnancy. Personal relationships suffer. Concentration and productivity at work decrease, and sexual dysfunction can happen. Also, there are psychological effects, such as feelings of shame and inadequacy.[7] And divorce is twice as likely to happen when porn is involved.[8]

Money is spent on pornography that could be used for household needs. And it takes you away from your duties and responsibilities, such as taking care of the home or spending time with the spouse or children. There is a cost, but there is no reward.

II. Are you thirsty for mind-altering substances?

Substance abuse: "Substance addiction and abuse is a complex disorder characterized by compulsive drug or alcohol use that leads to significant disruptions in daily living, including loss of work, relationships, and health."[9]

Abused substances cause intoxication. Intoxication lowers inhibition and alters judgment, perception, and attention. Physical control is sometimes lost. Substance abuse affects finances. "This includes $578 billion in economic loss and $874 billion dollars in societal harm through quality of life adjustment and premature loss of life." Health care cost, due to substance abuse, is $66 billion a year. It causes a decrease in productivity and an increase in crime.[10] Substance abuse affects our health, our finances, and our emotions. There is a cost, but there is no reward.

III. Are you thirsty for domestic violence?

Domestic violence "(also called intimate partner violence (IPV), domestic abuse or relationship abuse) is a pattern of behaviors used by one partner to maintain power and control over another partner in an intimate relationship. Domestic violence includes behaviors that physically harm, arouse fear, prevent a partner from doing what they wish or force them to behave in ways they do not want. It includes the use of physical and sexual violence, threats and intimidation, emotional abuse and economic deprivation."[11] Each minute in the United States, almost twenty people (close to 10 million a year) are abused by an intimate partner. Domestic violence hotlines receive more than 20,000 phone calls a day. Domestic violence costs more than $8.3 billion a year, and victims lose about 8 million days of work.[12]

[1,3]Lexico Dictionary. https://www.lexico.com/en/definition/thirsty/.

[2,4]Merriam-Webster Dictionary. https://www.merriam-webster.com/dictionary/thirsty/.

[5]Collins English Dictionary. https://www.collinsdictionary.com/us/dictionary/english/thirsty/.

[6]"Helping You to Preserve Family Values," Family Safe Media, accessed October 18, 2018, https://www.familysafe.com/pornography-statistics/.

[7]"An American Addiction Centers Resource," PsychGuides.com, accessed October 18, 2018, https://www.psychguides.com/behavioral-disorders/sex-addiction/.

[8]Schultz, David. ScienceMag.org. Aug 26, 2016. https://www.sciencemag.org/news/2016/08/divorce-rates-double-when-people-start-watching-porn#:~:text=For%20men%2C%20the%20chance%20of,from%205%25%20to%2010%25.&text=They%20note%20that%20when%20women,few%20stopped%20once%20they%20started/.

[9]"Addiction 101 Substance Abuse," Caron.org, accessed October 18, 2018, https://www.caron.org/understanding-addiction/defining-substance-abuse-addiction/.

[10]Recovery Centers of America, accessed October 18, 2018, https://recoverycentersofamerica.com/economic-cost-substance-abuse/

[11]National Domestic Violence Hotline, accessed October 18, 2018, https://www.thehotline.org/is-this-abuse/abuse-defined/.

[12]National Coalition Against Domestic Violence (NCADV), accessed October 18, 2018, https://ncadv.org/statistics?gclid=EAIaIQobChMI0PWY5Yfs6gIViobACh14IwYSEAAYASAAEgKOSfD_BwE

Abusive relationships tend to be cyclic: there's abuse, then reconciliation, then abuse, and then reconciliation again. Abusers are mainly seeking total control. They isolate you; they threaten you; they induce fear. The abused, on the other hand, are seeking love, validation, and security. They have low self-esteem, and they make excuses for the abuser. Some victims feel trapped because of fear or lack of finances. The abuser does not care about doing time in jail for assault or murder of a loved one. Jail time takes away income from the household. The abused suffers severe injuries, health problems, and mental problems. Children become aggressive, and they may grow up to become abusers or victims of abuse themselves. The costs are physical, financial, and emotional. There is a cost, but there is no reward.

When you are thirsty for Christ, for knowledge, for wisdom, and for right relationship, there is a cost, but there is also a reward. Your reward will be in heaven. When you keep God's commandments, when you live by the Beatitudes, when you produce the fruit of the spirit, your reward will be for eternity. Matthew 25:21 says, "His lord said unto him, Well done, thou good and faithful servant: thou hast been faithful over a few things, I will make thee ruler over many things: enter thou into the joy of thy lord."

Pornography, sex, substances that are abused, and power increase the level of dopamine in the brain. Dopamine is the primary neurotransmitter in the brain's reward center. Pleasure, however, is short-lived, but damnation is forever. Revelation 20:15 says, "And whosoever was not found written in the book of life was cast into the lake of fire."

The text tells us that Jesus broke from Jewish practices. First, Jesus went through Samaria, not around it. Second, he had a conversation with a woman. Jews did not talk to women for long periods of time because they believed it was a waste of time. They believed talking to women distracted them from studying scripture. Jesus knew the woman had a need, and he met her at her need and on her level. He met her where she was at. Many of us desperately try to fill that void ourselves, but that empty space remains empty because only Jesus can fill it. Jesus will give you what you need. You just have to ask for it. Matthew 7:7–8 says, "Ask, and it shall be given you; seek, and ye shall find; knock, and it shall be opened unto you: For every one that asketh receiveth; and he that seeketh findeth; and to him that knocketh it shall be opened." And Matthew 5:6 says, "Blessed are they which do hunger and thirst after righteousness: for they shall be filled." And you don't have to come up to his level; he will come down to yours. When you are thirsty for God, you will be fulfilled by God and you will receive God's reward. What are you thirsty for?

The Samaritan woman went to draw water after everybody else had left. She didn't want to run into Mother Judgmental or Evangelist Holier-Than-Thou or Deacon Self-Righteous or Reverend Critical. She just wanted water. She wanted to avoid the naysayers and the hypocrites. But Jesus knew what she was going to do. God knows your heart. He knows exactly what you are planning. He knows what you are going to do even before you do it. He knows you're about to get on the internet and watch porn, so Momma will call. He knows you're about to go buy some alcohol, so your sister will call. He knows you're about to make a booty call, so your brother will call. "Girl, what you doing? Boy, what you about to get into to?"

So what are you thirsty for today?

After service, as we walked out of the sanctuary, Kevin introduced me to several of his friends. They all seemed nice and accepting of me. But there were others who were not so welcoming. Some of the senior women seemed to turn their noses up at me, while the ladies my age rolled their eyes. I felt tension from these women, and I didn't understand it. I didn't know any of these people. What did they have against me?

Kevin took me to his friend's office. Bryson, the director of the men's ministry, Men after God's Heart, said, "Come on in. It's good to see you, man. I haven't seen you in about six months or so. Where have you been?"

"I had to take a sabbatical. Things started falling apart, and I needed to get away."

Kevin's other friends were there, and he introduced me to them: Bryson's wife Faye, and Chase and his wife Alaina. They all had gone to school together and were very close. They seemed like great people, and they welcomed me with open arms.

Lena, the church secretary sashayed into the room.

"What y'all up to?" she asked, grinning from ear to ear.

Immediately, my hot mess radar went off. Lena went straight for Kevin, and she was a little too smiley and too touchy-feely for me. When she put her arm around Kevin's waist to talk to him, I was very uncomfortable. I thought it was inappropriate and that Kevin should have said something. However, he didn't seem to mind at all. Guess he was too busy looking down at her double-Ds falling out of her blouse. "Nothing you need to concern yourself with," Chase said matter-of-factly.

"Humph," Lena responded.

As she walked away, she switched from east to west in her mid-thigh-high tight black skirt and her six-inch stilettos. I thought she was going to break a hip. She exuded sex. *Lord, please keep that woman away from my man. And keep my man away from her, too* I prayed.

"Girrrl," Alaina said, "you better keep your eye on that. She's been after him for years. She thought she was next in line after Emily."

"Who?"

"Emily, Kevin's ex-wife."

"Oh."

Afterward, Kevin invited me to his mom's house for dinner. He officially introduced me to everybody. They all seemed nice and seemed to accept me. He and his brothers kept something going. They enjoyed ribbing each other. I saw where Kevin got his competitiveness from. His mom loved to cook, and we had a feast. I loved the meatloaf, mashed potatoes and gravy, roasted corn, green beans, and biscuits. Everyone else pitched in with dessert. I was stuffed afterward and just wanted to take a nap. I ate so much that all I could do was sit on the couch and watch television with the rest of the family. Before I knew it, I had dozed off a few times. Kevin teased me about snoring and slobbering. "I did not!" I exclaimed. He laughed, and the rest of the family joined in.

I talked to Rochelle about her sermon and how I had really enjoyed it. She invited me to her women's group, Circle of Rubies, based on Proverbs 31. They met once a month on Thursday evenings. The older women mentored the younger women, and the married women mentored the single women. They all loved and supported each other. They took day trips for fun and fellowship, and she would love for me join them.

Kevin walked me to my car, and we said our goodbyes. I'd had a great time with his family. His parents were kind, and everyone had made me feel welcome.

CHAPTER 3

Lord, Is This Real?

On Valentine's Day, Kevin took me to a steakhouse for dinner. We talked about marriage and kids and our future together. Kevin already had two girls, and he wanted a son. He took hold of my hands and looked into my eyes. "Babe, I've never met anyone as special as you," he said. "You are the love of my life, and I want to spend the rest of it with you. I think about you all the time. I miss you so much when I'm not with you. I want us to be together permanently. I don't want to spend another day without you." After his passionate speech, Kevin stood up, reached into his pocket, and then got on one knee in front of me.

"Kayleigh, will you marry me?" he asked as he held up a beautiful diamond ring.

I was shocked. *He just got divorced and now he wants to get married again?*

"Kevin, I ..."

"Honey, please say yes. I love you. I know that you are the one for me."

Oh well, I thought, *if it doesn't work out, I'll just divorce him.*

"Yes," I said.

Kevin kissed me and hugged me. I thought he'd never let me go.

Later that night, I thought about Kevin's proposal and how we had met. I had asked the Lord for a friend. None of my relationships in the military had worked out. I was tired of being alone, and I wanted companionship. *Lord, is he the one?*

Kevin had told me some details of his divorce—but was that the whole story? Was it a mutual decision, or had he just walked away? Would he do the same to me? Deep down, I didn't want to know the truth. I was happy, and that was all that mattered in the moment. God had answered my prayer. Not only did I get a friend, but I got a husband, too.

I called my mom in South Carolina and told her everything. How I met Kevin, the lies he'd told, his justification for lying, that I believed he loved me, and that I loved him.

"So, you're just going to take his word for it?"

"Yes, ma'am. Why would he lie?"

"Why wouldn't he lie, child?"

"He said the marriage was over. He tried talking to her, but she wouldn't listen. She didn't want to be married. He's wasn't happy, and he wanted out."

"But what about her feelings? We as women give one hundred percent to relationships. We love with everything we have. We are all in when it comes to love. Do you really believe she wanted her marriage to end? Do you really believe she wanted to break up her family? They have how many kids?"

"Two."

"Would you want to lose your husband to another woman? Would you want someone to break up your family? Would you want your children to live without their father? Why don't you put yourself in her shoes?"

"But he said he loves me and wants to spend the rest of his life with me. He said I'm special, that he's never felt this way about anyone else. He said he doesn't want to live without me."

"Don't do it."

"But he loves me! How could that be wrong? I prayed for him, Momma."

"Baby, Satan will give you what you want, too. And God is not going to send you somebody else's husband. You need to walk away from this mess because it isn't right. It's not of God. He committed adultery, and you're fornicating. I brought you up better than that. You know the Word."

"I know, Momma, but I love him. I believe we can make it work."

"What if he were leaving you for her?"

I couldn't respond to that.

"Okay, baby. It's your decision. But remember, you reap what you sow."

"Okay, Momma. I love you."

"I love you, too, baby."

In June, Kevin and I were married. It was a small ceremony, with family and just a few close friends. Kevin's pastor, Rev.

David, performed the ceremony. Our mothers looked beautiful in their royal blue gowns. My mother seemed happy for me, but there was something else beneath the surface. Quiet disapproval? Two of my sisters and two of Kevin's sisters were bridesmaids. His friends were the groomsmen. His nephew was the ringbearer. I smiled as little Alex came bopping down the aisle in his tails. What a handsome young man!

We had the reception at an Italian restaurant.

For our honeymoon, Kevin and I flew to Hawaii for a week. We visited the Polynesian Cultural Center and enjoyed the presentations on the different cultures. And we went to Pearl Harbor. It was interesting to see the oil still bubbling up to the surface. The luaus were the best! They were awesome! Great local food, fun, and entertainment. We spent the days exploring the islands and the beaches. We spent the nights exploring each other.

After our honeymoon, Kevin and I bought a four-bedroom, three-bathroom ranch-style house. We were ready to start a family. Kevin and I attended church more regularly. We joined the couples' ministry, which Bryson and his wife Faye and Chase and his wife Alaina were already a part of. He joined the men's ministry with Bryson and Chase, and I joined the women's ministry with Faye and Alaina. Overall, things between Kevin and me were great. Every Friday was date night. We would do movies or bowling or skating or walks in the park. Every second Saturday, we had couples' night at the church, where we ate, played games, watched movies, and fellowshipped. We were planning a cruise for Christmas. Kevin still hung with his military buddies every weekend, and occasionally I and their wives would have "girls' night out."

We met another couple, Melvin and Gina, through Jake and Gina. This Gina, whom we started calling G2, loved to cook. Once a month, we all went to her and Melvin's house for some good ol' soul food or fish. We played cards and board games and always had a good time. They had a pool in the backyard, which we enjoyed, also.

At the end of every service, Kevin would speak to people on our way out. I stayed with him for about a month. After that, I couldn't take it anymore, and I started waiting for him in the car. There were some bold and desperate women in this church, with their short, tight skirts, plunging necklines, and high heels. Some of them completely ignored me and spoke at length to Kevin, holding his hand longer than necessary, batting their eyes at him, grinning from ear to ear. Kevin didn't say or do anything to deter them. As a matter of fact, he seemed to be enjoying the attention. He grinned back at them. He hugged them and kissed them on the cheek. The men patted him on the back. He came to the car on such a high. I didn't understand why he seemed to soak up the women's attention or why he needed men to pat him on the back, to validate him. Why did he need that?

I told Kevin how I felt about all those women fawning over him. I told him that it was inappropriate behavior and that it was disrespectful to me and to him. He said I was just being jealous and insecure.

I was a medical technologist in the chemistry department of the clinical laboratory at City Medical Center. There were seven of us on days. Three techs worked in main chemistry. Two techs worked in special chemistry. One tech worked urinalysis. And one tech floated. We rotated benches each week. Our supervisor, Kim, was wonderful. She was in her early fifties, and she was just as sweet as she could be. She often brought treats in for us. She reminded me of a grandmother. She cared about all of us. She really listened to our concerns and actually tried to make things better when there was a problem. We all got along like family. We were all respectful, responsible, and dependable. We didn't leave work or issues for other techs. We handled things as they came up. This was the best lab I'd ever worked in. I'd worked with plenty of lazy, incompetent techs, or techs who walked around socializing instead of working, or disappearing techs, in the past, but not in this department. Kim was nice, but strict and held each of us accountable for our actions.

I found a very good friend in Dennis. He was the only male in chemistry, and he was good people. He would give you the shirt off his back. He was hilarious, always talking about the rest of us. He didn't go behind our backs; he jokingly told us to our faces what he thought of us. We all loved him for being real. Dennis kept the atmosphere light, even when things got hectic. I had a job that I loved; I was getting paid to do something that I loved to do; I was truly blessed.

Dennis and I went to lunch together every day. He was a few years older than I was, and he became my big brother. He was very wise for his age. He made me rethink my views on men and women in general and on relationships. He had interesting points of view on all three subjects.

One day, I told Dennis about some of the women at church and how they came on to my husband in front of me.

"Sweetheart, let me tell you something. Some of them women ain't at church seeking Jesus. Some of them are seeking your husband," he said. "They're lonely and desperate, and they want a man, any man, your man. Chile, keep your husband close, and keep your eye on them hot tamales."

Kevin seemed to be enjoying his new job. Outside his office was his secretary's desk. I wasn't too keen on that. I met his secretary, Tamar. She looked okay, seemed nice. But I still didn't like her being so close to my husband. Shannon kept me up to date on everything happening in the ER. She told me about the women flirting with Kevin and wanting a piece of him. Kevin and I decided to keep our relationship private. We didn't want everyone in our business. We rarely ate lunch together or visited each other's department.

CHAPTER 4

Oh Lord, What Have I
Gotten Myself Into?

We got a new young member, Peggy, at church. She was unemployed, so Kevin helped her get a job at City Medical Center as an office assistant in the lab. Peggy was young and pretty with curves, and it didn't take long for the rumors to start that she and Kevin were having an affair. Shannon told me they would leave the hospital to go to lunch together. One of the techs in the ER lab said that Peggy was always in Kevin's face that and she had seen her lounging comfortably on the couch in his office. An acquaintance at Memorial Hospital told me he had seen them at a hotel downtown. Peggy came out of the room first and went to her car. Then Kevin came out and went to his car. Kevin was always at work. Work became his wife; I became his mistress.

Kevin loved to sing, and he joined the praise team. It wasn't long before Peggy joined, too. Now they were able to spend even more time together.

Rochelle and I grew close over the months, but we never discussed Kevin or my marriage. She was also on the praise team and was trying to recruit me, so I would drop by occasionally to see how they were doing. Several nights, I slipped in and just observed for a while. I saw how comfortable Peggy was with my husband. She seemed way too familiar with him. At times, I thought she was disrespectful. Kevin should have handled that, but, of course, he didn't. *Why does he keep letting women disrespect him in front of me? Why does he allow them to disrespect me?*

"Kevin, what's going on between you and Peggy?" I asked at home after a particularly suspicious interaction the two of them had at a praise team practice. I was fed up with watching them interact.

"Nothing, why?" he asked somewhat coldly.

"People are starting to talk about your behavior around her. She really needs to go. The city can help her find another job. What you're doing is inappropriate."

"We're just friends."

"Friends? You don't even know her. She's only been at the church a month and you're sniffing behind her, already. Stop it! Now! Or I will."

During the whole conversation, Kevin didn't look at me once. He kept fiddling with stuff on the dresser. I was talking to his back. Funny how he couldn't look me in the eye. Kevin and Peggy backed off from each other, and eventually she left the church and the job at the lab.

Dennis and I were having lunch one day. "You might want to go check on your man from time to time."

"We agreed to keep our distance at work. We want to keep things simple."

"Mmm." He looked at me pointedly. "You might want to go check on your man from time to time. It's not a good idea to leave your man unchecked or to leave your territory unmarked. Word is there's a new hot tamale in town and she takes no prisoners."

"What are you saying, Dennis?"

"I'm saying, Kay, go check on your man."

I left Dennis and went to Kevin's office. The door was closed. I knocked. "Come in," he said. I opened the door, took one step, and stopped. Little Miss Tart was sitting on his desk, comfortable as a Cheshire cat. He was leaning back in his chair, and she was propped up on the desk close to him with her legs crossed. My wifedar went into high alert.

"What's going on?" I asked.

"Oh, nothing, babe," Kevin said, standing up and coming toward me quickly. "Baby, this is Candy. She's the new charge nurse." Candy nodded my way. "We were just discussing an issue with samples being mislabeled. It's been happening more frequently, and she wanted some ideas on how to resolve the problem."

"Oh," I said. "And she needs to sit on your desk to do that? You have two perfectly good chairs right here," I said as I looked at her, raising my eyebrows.

Candy got off the desk and went toward the door. "We can

discuss this another time, Kev. I see you've got your hands full," she said sarcastically, looking at me.

Kev? Did she just call him Kev?

I closed the door gently as I took a deep breath. I wanted to slam it shut, but I had to remain professional. *"Kevin!* What is going on?"

"Nothing! We were just talking," he said exasperatedly.

"Why was she perched on your desk all comfortable? How often does she come in here? And 'Kev'? Why did she call you Kev? Nobody calls you that but me!"

"Will you calm down, please? Let's discuss this later at home, *okay?"*

After work, Shannon and I met for tea. We ordered, and as soon as we sat down, I pounced. "Who is Candy and why didn't you tell me about her?"

"I didn't want to go there. I know how much you love Kevin, and I really didn't see anything going on. My friend at Memorial Hospital said she's bad news, though. Her husband recently left her for a younger woman, so now she goes after married men. They asked her to leave Memorial, and she came here. She's been after Kevin hard, but he seemed to be holding his own. I did not think he would give in to her. He seems so committed to you."

At home, I asked Kevin about Candy. I told him what Shannon had said about her and voiced my concerns. "Baby, I love you and I am committed to you, to us. You don't have anything to worry about," he said.

At lunch the next day, I told Dennis what had happened. "Kevin said he was committed to me, to us."

"Girlfriend, he may be committed in his heart, but he's still a man, and some women will do anything to get him. Keep your man close and other women far away."

Eventually, Candy was transferred to the sixth floor. She wasn't a good fit for the emergency room, but her skills could be used elsewhere.

I didn't care very much for Kevin's secretary, Tamar, but over time she and I became friendly. She was from Pedro, also, and she and Kevin had known each other for a long time. Tamar would often call or text me for clarification on something when she couldn't get in touch with Kevin. Occasionally, we talked about other things. Tamar had been married and divorced three times. Two of her husbands had cheated on her and left her for younger, prettier women. She had two daughters with her first husband, but after the divorce, she had become seriously ill and was unable to care for them. They lived with her ex-husband in Culver, Texas. Tamar was an only child, and both her parents were dead. Dennis told me she had recently started dressing seductively after her third husband left. I sort of felt sorry for her.

One day in November, Tamar asked me to go to the mall with her on the upcoming Saturday morning to look for an outfit for the hospital's annual Christmas party. We did not find anything suitable, and at lunchtime, we decided to eat in the food court. After we finished eating, we were just sitting and talking when a woman came up to our table. She looked at me and pointed her finger.

"So, you married my husband, huh? Well, I hope he treats

you better than he treated me. He's nothing but a womanizer, sleeping with all them thirsty females. They thought I didn't know, but I did. See, people love to talk about other people's business. But you know what they say. What goes around comes around. I took him from his first wife. Yeah, he was with me before they divorced. He finally walked out on me two years ago this month. He didn't even have the nerve to tell me he was leaving. He just didn't come home one day. I see he didn't waste no time getting hitched again, though. I don't know why. He needs to stay single. Good luck, sister. You're going to need it," she said, smirking as she walked away.

His first wife?

Whaaat?

November? November? I asked myself, incredulously

So many thoughts were running through my mind.

He didn't say anything about two ex-wives.

And I met him in August. He was still with his second wife while he was seeing me??

He told me he was divorced. Then he said they were separated.

He lied to me. He … lied … to me …

Oh, no, what have I gotten myself into?

"Did you know about this?" I asked Tamar.

"Yeah. You didn't?"

"I had no idea."

"He was one of the biggest womanizers in town. He's very charming and charismatic. Women just fall for him. And his dimples. And that wavy black hair."

"Let's go," I said. Suddenly, I wasn't feeling well.

On the ride home, I thought about my situation. *When Kevin and I first met in August, he told me he was divorced. A month later, when I caught him in the lie, he said they were separated. She's saying he didn't move out until November. She has no reason to lie to me. So, he told me another lie to cover up the first lie. Why now?* I asked myself. *Why is she telling me this now? She obviously knew who I was and where I was. Why now?*

Kevin and I had been married over a year and were trying to have a baby. I couldn't undo what was already done. *I'll just have to deal with it*, I decided. I loved Kevin. I felt he loved me. We were happy. *I'm sure there's nothing to worry about. He won't cheat on me, too. He should be settled by now. He doesn't need other women. I'll be enough for him,* I tried to convince myself.

When I got home, Kevin was on the couch in the den watching a game on TV.

"Hey, honey. How was your day?" he asked.

"It was good," I answered. "How was yours?"

"Good. Didn't do anything. Tamar didn't walk you too much, did she?"

"No, we took breaks."

"You find anything?"

"No, nothing I liked."

"Well, you still have time."

"Yes. Do you want lunch?"

"No, thank you. I fixed a sandwich earlier."

"Oh, okay. Tamar and I ate at the food court."

I decided not to tell him about the conversation I'd had with his *second* ex-wife.

"I'm kind of tired. Going to lie down for a while."

"Okay, honey," he said as he got up and kissed me on the forehead.

Later that night, Kevin wanted to make love to me. I wasn't feeling it at all, given the new knowledge I had, but I couldn't deny him. The Bible says in 1 Cor. 7:4–5 that my body is not mine, but his, and that I should not withhold sex. I performed to the best of my ability with his lies on my mind, hoping that he didn't notice anything was amiss. Afterward, he asked, "Honey, are you okay?"

"Yes, babe. Just a little tired, still."

He lay on his back and pulled me into his arms. I laid my head on his chest, hoping he would go to sleep fast so I could roll over away from him. I decided to forgive Kevin for the lies and deception. There was nothing I could do now, anyway. I moved past my skepticism and fears. I worked hard to make my marriage as happy and successful as possible. I wanted a son, and I wanted my family to stay together. I prayed for Kevin, for me, and for us.

Over time, Tamar and I got closer. She would ask me over to her house for lunch on Saturdays. Sometimes, we went to the mall. Tamar kept me up to date on the latest gossip. She knew everybody's business. Everybody seemed to confide in her. I even ended up saying some things about Kevin and me.

"Well, if you ever need to get away, you can stay with me," she offered.

CHAPTER 5

Lord, Give Me Strength

Kevin and I had decided to keep our marriage low-key at work, so we did not often eat lunch or spend a lot of time together there. I decided to start checking up on him, so occasionally, I would find a reason to go downstairs to the ER. Kevin introduced me to Chloe, a new RN. Immediately, my spirit was uneasy with her. For the first two weeks, every time Chloe saw me, she would come up to me and make small talk. Was she really trying to be my friend, or was she up to something? Suddenly, all that friendliness stopped, however; instead, she chose to talk only to my husband.

One Friday around lunchtime, I saw Kevin and Chloe talking. She had on skintight black leather pants, and she had him pinned in the corner. I shook my head. Shannon told me later she had stopped by on her day off. *Here we go again.*

I woke up Saturday morning feeling very excited. Tonight, I was going to strut my stuff. Tonight was my night to shine.

It was the annual Christmas party at work. This year, it was a formal affair at the country club. I walked into the banquet room on my husband's arm. He had on a black tuxedo with a royal blue bowtie and cummerbund. I had on a royal blue gown with matching pumps and purse. We went to our table and discussed the highlights of the week and the expectations of the night. When he looked at me and smiled, my heart still melted. I loved those dimples! And the thin mustache and trimmed goatee. And the sexy, short, wavy hair. He was so handsome! And I was proud to be with him.

The host got the program started with words of welcome. A dance group entertained us. There was a comedienne and a couple of soloists; then dinner was served. As we were being served, I noticed Chloe staring at my husband. She was seated at the table directly across from our table, and she had been watching us all evening. Now she was staring. She had this look of pain and disappointment on her face.

"Babe," I said to my husband, "why is she staring at you?"

"I don't know," he said fidgeting and looking uncomfortable.

Kevin looked at her, and something passed between them. He dropped his arm from around my shoulder, and he physically shifted away from me.

OMG! No, he didn't!

I looked at him with a question on my face, but he didn't say anything. He looked so guilty; then he looked away. My guard went up immediately.

What's going on here? I asked myself.

I looked at her again, and she was still staring at him. I looked at him, and he was staring at her.

Lord, help me, I prayed.

I went to the bathroom to freshen up after dinner, and I ran into my friend Shannon.

I told her about the looks between Kevin and Chloe, and she dropped her eyes.

"What?" I asked.

She didn't respond.

"What?" I asked again.

"That's her," she said.

"Her who?" I asked.

"Your husband's latest conquest."

My mouth dropped open.

"What do you mean, 'latest conquest'?"

"He's been seeing her since shortly after she got here."

"Why didn't you tell me?"

"Cameron told me to stay out of it." Cameron was Shannon's boss, and the two of them were close. "He talked to your husband, but it didn't do any good. And I didn't want to hurt you."

"How do you know?"

"She's in his office a lot for one reason or another. They go to lunch together. She comes to see him on her days off, and sometimes she brings him lunch. They are in his office alone. Cameron and I both told Kevin about being in his office alone with women, but you know how Kevin is. He doesn't listen to anybody. Thinks he can do whatever he wants. I'm sorry,

Kayleigh. I just couldn't tell you," Shannon told me while trying to comfort me with a hug.

I made it through the rest of the night watching them stare at each other. All night, she stared at him, looking hurt; he stared at her, looking guilty. I was sick to my stomach, but I made it through. *God, give me strength,* I prayed over and over. Smokie Norful's song, "I Need You Now" played in my head, and I was comforted by that.

Later that night, after Kevin went to bed, I got his phone and scrolled through the call log.

Chloe.

Chloe.

Chloe …

Three hours for this call, two hours for that call, several times a day, every day.

I checked the text messages.

From tonight:

Chloe: "How could you do this to me?!! I was supposed to be on your arm tonight. You said she wasn't going! I'm tired of being on the side. I want people to know about us."

Kevin: "Babe"—*(Babe? He calls me Babe!)*—"I'm sorry. She said she didn't feel well. But she got better. What was I supposed to do? I'm sorry. I promise I'll make it up to you."

Chloe: "You better! Or I'll put this on lock!"

Kevin: "No, baby. Don't do that, now."

Yesterday:

Kevin: "Thinking about you."

(Really? I thought.)

Chloe: "Thinking about you too, sweet thang."

Kevin: "When can I see you again? I love when you wear that leather cat suit and drop it like it's hot in those stilettos."

Chloe: "Anytime you want, honey. Just holla."

The messages went on and on. He was so cocky he hadn't even bothered deleting anything.

I saw red. I went to the garage and grabbed the hammer out of his toolbox. I took the hammer and the phone to the guest bathroom. I put the phone on the counter. I grabbed the hammer, covered my eyes with my left hand, and started hitting the phone with all the force I could muster.

The glass shattered. The plastic broke. By the time I finished, that phone was totally destroyed. It was a mangled mass of glass and plastic. Kevin won't be cheating on this phone anymore.

I slept on the couch that night. I was too angry to deal with him. Sunday morning, I got up and started dressing for church. Bishop John was preaching for Men's Day. That man was anointed, and I loved to hear him deliver the Word. He lived what he preached. He had only been in the area a year, but his reputation had preceded him. Bishop John didn't play. He was quick to cut a preacher down if there was even a hint of impropriety. All the pastors were afraid when he called their names in meetings, but they respected him. Other bishops let their pastors do anything. As long as the money was coming in, the bishops looked the other way, especially in the "good old boys" club.

I came out of the bathroom, and Kevin was waiting for me.

"What did you do to my phone? Have you lost your mind?"

I knew it was coming, the argument, and I was prepared.

"No, but you have! I know about you and Chloe, about the lunch dates, about you leaving work. I saw the phone log and the texts. You should be ashamed of yourself!"

"We're just friends!" he yelled. "And I'm helping her with a problem."

"Really?" I responded. "Kevin, I'm not blind. You've been disappearing for a couple of months now. I didn't say anything because I really believed you were working."

His eyes fell.

"You can't seem to make it home before midnight lately, and I saw the way she looked at you last night." He dropped his head.

"That is not just friendship, and you will shut it down immediately or you and I can discuss it with Alice next week." Alice was the laboratory director, and she was big on professionalism and morality. She had fired someone last week for inappropriate posts on social media. We had had a lab meeting, and she had set the standards she expected us to adhere to, supervisors even more so.

His shoulders slumped, and suddenly he was calm. "There's nothing to tell Alice. I said we're just friends."

"Then out of respect for your wife, please stop all communication with her."

Kevin turned away from me and started playing with the dresser items again.

"You've crossed the line, and there's no going back. If she

needs help, employee assistance is available and more than capable. And they know how to keep it in their pants."

"But ..." he started, half turning toward me.

"It ends now," I said, and I walked to my closet. Funny how he couldn't keep eye contact with me.

Bishop John really brought it that morning! His subject was "A Way of Escape." His text was 1 Cor. 10:13. He talked about temptation and how Satan uses your weaknesses against you.

"Satan will set you up and make you look like a fool. He will make you betray God and yourself. You will betray the very thing that you love most—your ministry, your spouse, your family and friends—to get what Satan is dangling in front of you. But my God says he will help you out. He says he will provide a way of escape. He has the escape route, but you have to be willing to use it. David can tell you, 'For he that soweth to his flesh shall of the flesh reap corruption' (Gal. 6:8). Samson can tell you, 'For the wages of sin is death' (Rom. 6:23). Saints, you will get yourself in trouble with God when you keep going your way."

After service, I saw my friend Gina from the couples' ministry.

"Girl, what's wrong with your husband? Jake"—(her husband)—"said he was bent over bawling." Kevin and Jake had sat with the men for the Men's Day service.

"Really?"

"Yeah, girl. He cried like a baby when Bishop started preaching. What'd you do to that man last night?"

"I didn't do anything. Maybe he finally got a conscience."

Kevin seemed to straighten up after Chloe. She was terminated for making too many mistakes. For a while, Kevin spent more time at home. He surprised me with flowers. He was more loving toward me. I forgave him, again, and we were on the road to recovery.

Evangelist Rochelle did a two-night revival, and Kevin and I recommitted our lives to Christ. The first night, she preached from Josh. 2:1–21 and Josh. 6:21, 25: "I Don't Want to Live Like This Anymore." She told the story of Rahab.

"Some scholars say Rahab was an innkeeper. The Bible says she was a harlot, a prostitute. We don't know her history or what got her on that path. Today, there are several reasons why a woman ends up in prostitution. Maybe she was abused as a child by her father or her uncle or someone else she should have been able to trust to protect her. Maybe her mother or father put her out of the house and she had to make her own way. Maybe she was running away from her mother's abusive boyfriend and ran into John, who she thought would help her and take care of her, but instead he used her and abused her, too. So, Rahab was a prostitute, but somewhere along the way, she heard about God. She heard how God had dried up the Red Sea. She heard how God had helped the Israelites destroy two great kings. She recognized that God was sovereign both in heaven and on earth. She knew that God could save her life and that of her family. She believed that he would. She risked her life by hiding the spies; then she lied to the king. She did not fear the king; she feared God. Yes, the king would have spared her life if she had given up the spies, and he might would have rewarded her. But God is the ultimate savior. He is the ultimate rewarder. God will save your soul and offer you eternal life.

"So, it doesn't matter where you are in life tonight. It doesn't matter what you have done. Don't worry about the folk in the church building. They are not a part of the church; they are just in the building perpetrating Christianity, disguised as Christians, wearing the mask of a Christian. God will deal with them later. The Bible says in Matt. 21:31 that even the harlot will make it into the kingdom of heaven before these hypocrites will. Tonight, you can be saved. Tonight, God can change your life. Are you tired of being tired? Are you sick of being sick? Allow God to change your life. Allow God to save your soul. Allow God to offer you eternal life. You don't have to *live* like this anymore. You don't *have* to live like this anymore."

The second night, she preached about the woman with the issue of blood found in Luke 8:43–48 and Mark 5:25–34. Her subject was, "How Bad Do You Want it?"

"As Jesus was on his way to heal Jairus's daughter, he was interrupted. Someone got his attention, and he had to stop. There was a woman who had had an issue of blood for twelve long years. She had spent all of her money on doctors who could not heal her. She actually grew worse. Can you imagine spending a lot of money on doctors and tests and procedures and actually getting worse? How frustrating! How disheartening! But one day, she heard about Jesus. She heard the master was passing through. She knew that he could heal her. She believed that he would heal her, if she could only touch him. Just a touch.

I can imagine her talking to herself. "I'm on my knees, but I have to get there. I have to crawl, but I have to get there. I have to fight the crowd, but I have to get there. I need a touch. I need a touch. I know he can. I need a touch. I believe he will. I need a touch. They're talking about me, but I need a touch. They're laughing at me, but I need a touch. They're pushing me back, pushing me away, but I need a touch. They're trying to discourage me. They're hating on me. *But I need a touch!* Whatever it takes.

Whatever I have to do. Wherever I have to go. I need a touch! I heard about him. They said he healed the sick and he raised the dead. They said he made a blind man see and he made a deaf man hear. They said he made a lame man walk and he called out demons from another man. If he did it for them, I believe he will do it for me. I have to get there! I need a touch!"

She got down low and touched his garment and was healed immediately. Jesus asked, "Who touched me?" She was afraid, but she stepped forward anyway, fell down before him, and confessed. How bad do you want it tonight? Do you need healing, deliverance, peace, a financial blessing? Are you willing to humble yourself before God and cry out to him? He already knows your needs, but he's waiting on you to come to him. He's not going to force himself on you. It's your choice. Will you choose him, tonight? He is a healer. He is a deliverer. He is a way maker, a miracle worker. He is all that you need. How bad do you want it?

"With all the people around him, she made her way to him. She was considered unclean, but she risked rejection and punishment to get to Jesus. She wasn't supposed to be around anyone, but she wanted healing badly enough to take a chance. She'd tried everything else; now it was time to try Jesus. She pushed down pride, forced down fear, and made her way to Jesus. Will you make your way to Jesus tonight? How bad do you want what you need? How bad do you want it?"

Many people were healed, delivered, and saved. Evangelist Rochelle was one anointed woman of God!

CHAPTER 6

Lord, Please Help Me

By the time Christmas came around, I was looking forward to spending some quality time with my husband. He had gotten busy again with work and the church and was spending a lot of time away from home. We went to my mother-in-law's house for dinner. I could hardly wait to get into that turkey and dressing, cranberry sauce, macaroni and cheese, potato salad, collard greens, cabbage, corn on the cob, chocolate cake, strawberry shortcake, pineapple upside down cake, apple pie, peach cobbler, potato pie ... I always enjoyed going to mom-in-law's house. Kevin's brothers were so crazy. They always talked junk. And his sisters could hate on other women like nobody I've ever seen. They would dissect a sister from head to toe, from weave to stilettos. I ate and laughed so much my stomach hurt.

Kevin and I had been married for seven years now and still had not conceived.

After dinner, we were sitting around shooting the breeze when I got an email notification on my phone.

Who would be emailing me on Christmas day?

To: Wifey@mail.com
From: Sidechick@mail.com
Subj: Your husband is a liar and a cheater

Dear Wifey,

I really hate to tell you this, but your husband is a liar and a cheater. He is sharing himself with so many other women. I thought I was the only side dish, but apparently, he likes variety. We had been sleeping together for two years, and now he's with somebody else. And there have been others besides her. He's been lying to you, me, and them.

I called my husband outside and showed him the email.

"What is this?" I asked. He read the email.

"I don't know anything about that. Somebody's lying on me. They are just jealous and trying to start something," he said, looking past me.

Funny how he couldn't look me in the eye.

Lord, what is going on? What is wrong with this man? Does he want to lose everything? Why is he so foolish?

I thought older meant wiser. Lord, it's in your hands.

"The pieces of the puzzle will be revealed," he whispered in response.

Six months later, in June, I got a text from Sandy, the leader of the young ladies' club at church. Pretty in Pink was for girls ages fifteen to eighteen, and it helped young girls transition into young ladies. She had recently given birth to the prettiest little boy. He was about ten months old now. She was engaged, and she and her fiancé had twin girls together. I couldn't wait to have my son; there was just something about a mother-and-son relationship that made me want it so badly.

Sandy: Mrs. Kayleigh. I really need to talk to you.

Me: What about?

Sandy: About Kevin.

Me: What about him?

Sandy: Can we just talk in person, please?

Me: Okay. Come by the house tomorrow evening. He has a meeting.

Sandy: Okay.

Sandy came over around 4:00 p.m. I led her into the den and offered her something to drink. She declined.

"Okay, Sandy, what's going on?"

"Kevin and I have been sleeping together for the past two years."

"Wh ... What?"

I was stunned. This girl had to be twenty years his junior.

"We've been sleeping together for the past two years," she repeated. "And he is the father of my son."

She handed me a piece of paper—DNA test results.

The alleged father, Kevin, cannot be excluded as the

biological father of the child named Keyvonne. Based on testing results obtained from analyses of fifteen different DNA probes, the probability of paternity was 99.9999%.

The paper fell from my hand.

"How did this get started?" I asked as I watched the paper lying on the floor, waiting for the words to change to something else.

"He came on to me after choir rehearsal one night when you were visiting your mom. She was sick, and you were gone for a couple weeks. He would make sexual comments like, 'Your man home tonight? Because if he isn't, I can fill in.'

"Then he started texting me stuff. 'When can we meet? I want to get with you.'"

"How often were you together?"

"Once or twice a week. He would text me, 'I want to see you.'"

"What about your fiancé?"

"He works two jobs, so he's gone most of the time."

"Did my husband bring you into my home?"

"Yes, downstairs in the basement."

"And my bed?"

"No."

"So, why are you telling me this, now?"

"I just think you should know. He should be stopped."

"Why didn't you come to me two years ago, *before* it got started?"

"I didn't think it would go anywhere. I thought he was just playing. Then he said you two were having problems and that you weren't sleeping together. He said you were getting divorced."

"So, you sent that email to me on Christmas?"

"Yes."

After a few moments of silence, I said, "I think you should leave now."

"Mrs. Kayleigh, I'm really sorry. I didn't mean to hurt you."

"But you did. Now leave."

She put her hand on the door handle and then looked back at me.

"He's seeing Tamar now. She said he's going to marry her," she said.

I felt like I had been punched in the gut. Tamar was supposed to be my friend.

"So, is that why you're telling me all this? Because he dumped you for her? *Really*? Why would you tell me now that he broke it off with you? I didn't know about you. He got away with it. Oh, I get it. He hurt you, and you don't want him to get away with it. You want to hurt him like he hurt you. Did you consider that you would hurt me, too? I didn't even know about you. Oh, you want to do the right thing? *Now* you want to do the right thing? What about two years ago? Why didn't you do the right thing then and walk away? You knew he had a wife. You saw us together at church on Sundays. And what about your family? You jeopardized your family as well. What if I tell your fiancé?"

After Sandy left, I got on my knees and cried out to God as mournful sobs wracked my body.

Lord, help me.

Lord, help me.

God, I need you right now. Give me strength, Lord.

Give me peace. Lord, you work this out. Lord, show me what to do.

Jesus.

Jesus.

Jesus.

Jesus.

Jesus.

My world was just shattered into a million pieces. I was shocked. I was lost. I couldn't believe what had just happened. I couldn't comprehend that he had done it again. *Why, Lord? Why?*

I had felt in my spirit that something was wrong. But those were just feelings. They were just suspicions. They weren't really real. As long as there was no proof, it wasn't real, right? As long as there was no evidence, there was still hope. Right? I hoped that my husband still loved me. I hoped that he still wanted me. I hoped that he was still committed to the sacred vows he had made to me before God. Well tonight, I came face to face with proof. Tonight, it became real. My husband was giving himself to other women. My husband was cheating *on* me the same way he had cheated *with* me.

Kevin came home just before midnight. He showered and came to bed. As I lay next to him, the tears fell. I cried silently for my husband, who was lost, for my marriage, which was broken, and for myself, who was confused and in so much pain. *How did this happen?* I asked myself. *How did we get here?*

Over time, Kevin was gone more than he was home. Our Friday date night ended at some point. I don't even remember when or why. He stopped calling me "babe" and "honey." He didn't address me at all. He just said what he had to say and walked away. He hadn't looked me in the eye in a long time. Our sex life slowly diminished. Kevin stopped initiating sex. The few times that I wanted to, he turned me down.

"Not tonight, Kay. I'm tired."

"Not tonight. I had a long day."

Now I knew why he was so tired. Now I knew the real reason his days were so long. He had been putting all of his energy into other women.

I couldn't go to work the next day. I called out sick. My friend Dennis texted me later in the morning.

Dennis: Are you okay? Heard you called out.

Me: No. Kevin is cheating on me.

Dennis: Girl, I am so sorry.

Dennis: Is he home?

Me: No. He's at work.

Dennis: I'll be right there.

Me: What??

Dennis: I said I'll be right there.

Dennis was at my house twenty minutes later. I opened the door in my pajamas and robe. We sat on the couch.

"How did you get away?" I asked.

"I told Kim I had a family emergency." Kim was our supervisor.

"Oh."

"Girl, I am so sorry. How did you find out?"

"Sandy told me."

"That homewrecker."

"You know her?"

"Yes. She's been around the block a few times. You didn't know Kevin was cheating?"

"No. Did you?"

"Let's be real now, Kay. You didn't know Kevin was cheating?"

"I had my suspicions. I just didn't want to accept it."

"Yes. People are talking about it. Say he's got a baby by one of them."

"One of them? How many are there?"

"Only heard about two, Sandy and Tamar."

I started bawling. He pulled me to him and held me in silence while I cried. After at least half an hour, I was able to calm down and breathe normally.

"I hate to say this, but you know me. I tell it like it is. Once a cheat, always a cheat. Weren't you the mistress at one time? Honey, men like that don't change. They are just good at covering their tracks. If he cheated with you, sooner or later he was going to cheat on you. But don't worry about him. You don't need that mess in your life. You deserve better. Girlfriend, men treat you the way you allow them to treat you. You really need to let him go. He wasn't yours to begin with anyway."

"But we just recommitted our lives to God."

"Girlfriend, your husband may be a man of God, but he's a man first."

Dennis stayed with me a while longer. When he was sure that I was going to be okay, he left. I felt so much better. I felt release. I felt cleansed. I read somewhere that tears clear the body of toxic chemicals. The way I'd cried, my body was cleansed of everything! As I prayed, peace came over me. I was still deeply hurt, but I knew that God was going to make everything okay.

Monday morning, I walked into Kevin's office and stopped short. Tamar was behind his desk, straightening his tie. She saw me and jumped back. I didn't say anything. I turned around and left. I was not going to stoop to their level. *Lord, give me strength.*

I did not talk to my husband about the conversation I had had with Sandy. Every night, I put it before God. *Lord, fix it.*

For the next two weeks, Kevin came in the house every night just before midnight. I didn't ask where he had been. I knew. I smelled her perfume as he made his way to the bathroom to shower. Eventually, he started sleeping on the couch, and then he moved into the guest bedroom. Every night, I cried myself to sleep. I loved my husband dearly, and I wanted our marriage to work, but he had to want it as well. Some mornings when I turned the TV on in the den, Cinemax or Playboy popped up. He was into porn as well. There's nothing on Cinemax at night but sex.

CHAPTER 7

Lord, Let Your Will Be Done

Four weeks after my conversation with Sandy, Kevin moved out. He said he needed to be alone and figure out some things. He said he wasn't happy, and this marriage wasn't working for him. Two weeks later, I was served with divorce papers. Two months later, I was divorced.

So, what are people going to think about me now? Did I fail as a wife? Did I not do my "wifely duties" enough? Is that why he turned to someone else? And what about my feelings? Am I supposed to feel more like his sexual outlet than his wife? Am I supposed to accept his jumping into bed and wanting sex? Shouldn't I get a note by my purse in the morning before I leave for work saying "I love you"? Shouldn't I get a text during the day saying "Thinking of you"? Shouldn't I get a hug when he comes in the door and a "Baby, how was your day?" Shouldn't I get a foot massage every now and then? Can't we go on a date sometime? Or am I just the wife who cooks his dinner, cleans his house, and opens my legs when he gets ready? What about me?

What about my feelings? What about my needs? He wants sex; I want love. If he takes care of my emotional needs, I'll take care of his physical needs. That's fair, right?

I talked to Kim about everything that had happened between Kevin and me and I resigned from City Medical Center. I kept in touch with Shannon and Dennis, however, and they both told me about Kevin's plans to marry Tamar. Gina, Sara, Rachel, and I still had girls' night out occasionally. They were very supportive.

As I reflected on my marriage, I realized there were a lot of things we should have done differently. We should have prayed for and with each other. We should have put God first, each other second, and ourselves third. If he had taken care of me as I took care of him, then we both would have been taken care of.

There were red flags at the beginning of the relationship. There were signs—bright neon signs—all of which I ignored. I looked the other way. Had sex not been in the equation, I would have seen them clearly. I bonded with someone who was not my husband. My emotions got in the way of reason.

Marriage is not always easy, but it's worth it. It's worth fighting for. Remember what you saw in her when you first fell in love with her. Remember how you felt about her when you decided "she's the one," when you thought, *I don't want to live without her in my life.* Find a way to get back to that place. Rekindle the fire. Remember! Remember!

I almost let go. I could have been dead. I should have been dead. I would have been dead by now had Satan had his way …

---

but God! God blocked it. God said, "You shall not die, but live, and declare the works of the Lord" (Psa. 118:17). God said, "For I know the thoughts that I think toward you, saith the Lord, thoughts of peace, and not of evil, to give you an expected end" (Jer. 29:11).

One night, after my divorce was finalized, I lay in bed drowning in my tears. I didn't want to watch TV. I didn't want to read a book. I didn't want to pray. I didn't want to read my Bible. As the tears flowed uncontrollably, my thoughts turned to suicide. *If I can just get out of bed and make it to the kitchen, it will all be over*, I thought. *I have a bottle of pills I can take. I will just go to sleep and it will all be over.*

I didn't really want to die. I knew that suicide was a sin. I knew I was going to hell if I did it, but I didn't care. I just wanted the excruciating pain to end. I didn't want to feel the humiliation anymore. I didn't want to see the images in my mind anymore of him and Sandy and him and Tamar. I didn't want to imagine them laughing and talking about me. There was no other option in those moments of deep distress. It had to end now. I had to do it.

I had been married for seven years. Now I was divorced, alone, and lonely. I had lost everything. I had built my life around my husband. Now, I had lost my mate, my identity. Now, I had to start all over. On top of that, my husband's mistresses were acquaintances, people whom I saw on a regular basis. They were people who I had thought respected me. And Tamar ... my friend? My friend took my husband from me. As all of this began to sink in, it tore me apart. The shame, the humiliation, the betrayal, and the pain were unbearable.

Not my husband.

Not me.

This was not happening to me.

He used to tell me I was the love of his life. Then why did he need her? He used to say he loved me with all of his heart. So why did he break mine? He used to say he loved me to death. Well, I'm dying now. The man whom I loved dearly, whom I looked up to, whom I had shared a bed with at one time, had been sharing himself with others. The man by whom I desperately wanted a son gave my son to another woman, and she was flaunting it in my face. She was eager to give me details about her affair with my husband and her coming to my house and his going to her house. He had shared personal information about me with her, and she was happy to inform me. After our last anniversary celebration, he had told her it wasn't going to work. Why was he talking to her about me and our marriage instead of talking to me about her and why he felt the need to have her in his life? She wanted me to know that he would text her "I want to see you." Almost every Sunday, Sandy was in the choir loft singing the songs of Zion. I had felt so proud of her.

And Tamar ... how could she stab me in the back like this? All the phone calls and lunches and confidential conversations were just an entry point for her into my marriage. She had used the information I gave her against me.

And my husband ... They all looked me in my face knowing they were sharing a bed. I felt like such a fool. *Kevin obviously didn't use protection. He put my health at risk. How could he be so foolish as to pick up trash off the street? How could he be so selfish as to bring that trash into our home and then deposit it into me?* The more I thought about this mess, the more the pain flowed. The more the pain flowed, the more the tears flowed. The more the pain and tears flowed, the more the suicidal thoughts flowed.

Do it.

Nobody cares.

Nobody will miss you.

God doesn't really care about you.

Where is he now that you need him? He doesn't love you, or he wouldn't have let this happen. Look at you. You're a mess. You're pathetic.

I had been praying for a son—a son to bond with, to follow in his father's footsteps. That was my plan; it obviously was not God's plan. *Lord, why me? How could this happen to me? He said he loved me. God, how could you allow this to happen to me? Didn't I serve you enough? Don't you love me, God? How can you love me and allow this to happen? What did I do to deserve this? God, are you there? Are you there, God?*

As I was letting go of God's hand, he was still holding onto mine. I picked up the phone and called my friend Gina to take me to the hospital. She came right away and didn't ask any questions. In the car, I told her some of what I was feeling through my bouts of crying. I was such an emotional mess that I was shaking. She talked to me during the ride to keep my mind off my situation.

I was processed pretty quickly and taken to an examination

room, where an angel was waiting for me. The nurse, Troy, took my vitals and got the reason for my visit to the emergency room. After letting me talk for a bit, Troy began to minister to me. As he began to speak, I knew it was God. God had not abandoned me after all. Troy told me that he was not usually at this hospital, but they needed help and had pulled him from his other duty station. I knew that God had placed him there for me. He reminded me of God's love for me and gave me reasons to live. He encouraged me and told me that I didn't need that man (my ex-husband) in my life anyway. I deserved better than that. God had so much more in store for me. Troy even hugged me when he finished.

I spent seven days in a behavioral health facility. They gave me the tools that I needed to accept my new reality and the strength to start the healing process.

Nothing on this earth is worth your life. First of all, life is a precious gift from God, and it's not ever yours to take. Suicide is a rejection of God's gift. It's saying to God, "I don't want this gift anymore. You can have it back." Yes, life may be difficult, and it may seem like you can't make it, but I'm a living witness that you can. God will never leave you nor forsake you. Satan is on his job of stealing, killing, and destroying, twenty-four/seven. He will discourage you and make you feel like your only option is to die. He will make you feel that God doesn't love you, that God has abandoned you. Satan is a master at mind games. Suicide, however, is *not* an option. God loves you, and he will take care of you. He will be with you in the storm. He will carry you through the storm, if you let him. You have to trust him. Trust God!

Today, my story is for God's glory. Hallelujah! I almost let go, but God! God stepped in right on time. The devil thought he had me, but the devil is a liar! As Christians, we will experience many trials and tribulations, but God will always see us through. I praise God for bringing me through that mess. He turned my trial into triumph. He turned my test into a testimony. All glory to God!

CHAPTER 8

Lord, I Thank You

Shannon called me one day. "Hey, how have you been?"

"I'm surviving."

"Have you heard about Kevin?"

"Heard what?"

"He got fired."

"Really? What happened?"

"He started messing with some other chick, and Tamar went crazy. Then Sandy brought her son to the job, and Tamar really lost it. They fired both of them. I'm sure Sandy just wanted Kevin to acknowledge his son, the child they created together. Tamar told Sandy to get her child out of the office, and Sandy and Tamar got into it and had to be physically separated. They were both arrested. I'm quite sure Tamar was just jealous because she didn't have a child with Kevin. They have been at each other for a while now. Tamar even took out a restraining order against Sandy. I don't understand why they are fighting each other. They were both doing the same thing; they were both involved with a married man. Anyway, word got back to Alice, and the rest is history."

Oh, what a tangled web we weave. Look at the lies unraveling. He thought he had all the bases covered. He thought he had it all under wraps. Look at truth stepping in, I thought.

"Well, Kevin should have acknowledged his son. When you bond with someone other than your wife and create a life, don't punish the child. Denying that child does not change the facts. The child is yours. Denial doesn't make the situation go away. Take care of your responsibility. You were man enough to create a child outside of your marriage; be man enough to take care of it. That child deserves to have both of his parents in his life, just as your other children do."

"Tamar called off the wedding. Kay, please know that what he did had nothing to do with you. You were a good wife and would have been a great mother. He was broken."

Was? I thought.

"He had some baggage, some hurt from his past that he never dealt with. He just carried it from one relationship to the next, hoping it would go away. He has a void, and he is trying to fill it with women and sex instead of filling it with Jesus. Sooner or later, he's going to have to face himself. Sooner or later, he's going to get tired of looking at that man he sees in the mirror. Sooner or later, he's going to get tired of running from himself.

"I believe that he thought he loved you, but the truth is, he couldn't love you because he doesn't even love himself. He doesn't love himself because he doesn't know God's love, and he's not capable of loving anyone else. He is weak and he is broken. He lied to you. He betrayed you. He disrespected you. He dishonored you and God. But God will take care of you if you trust him."

"Thank you, Shannon."

Kevin was finished in this town. Why did he let his manhood get in the way? He had everything—a great job, a beautiful wife— and he threw it all away. And for what? A few seconds of pleasure? Used goods? Wonder if he thinks it was worth it now.

Dennis and Shannon encouraged me to ask for my job back. I called Kim and went back to City Medical Center.

RECOVERY

This book is a work of fiction based on some things that happened in my life. Some details have been changed, but the basic facts remain.

1. I got involved with a married man and eventually married him.
2. He cheated on me the same way he cheated on his ex-wife.
3. God brought me through the pain, even though I created the mess. His grace and his mercy endure forever.

My recovery from a broken heart was long and difficult, but God pulled me through. So many people betrayed my trust. My biggest obstacle, however, was forgiving myself. I honestly believed God had sent me my husband, but at the same time, I went against my faith. I was taught that remarriage was not possible after divorce, yet I married a man who had been divorced twice. People rarely change. History often repeats itself. If he did it to her, chances are he will do it to you.

I forgave my ex-husband and the other women in his life

who knew he had a wife and family and did not care. They chose to get involved with him anyway. I was depressed. I was suicidal. I was angry with God, and at times, I hated God. How could he do this to me? We have to take responsibility for our actions. What you put out there will come back to you. "Be not deceived; God is not mocked: for whatsoever a man soweth, that shall he also reap" (Gal. 6:7). But God is faithful to help us even when we get ourselves in trouble. He loves us. He cares about us.

I blamed myself. I hated myself. But I had to realize that we all make mistakes. We all make bad choices. We must learn from them and keep it moving. I learned from my mistakes, and I want to help others through the pain of a broken heart from a broken relationship. I want to encourage you to get counseling and take medication, if necessary.

Whatever you need to do to make *you* better, do it. Don't be ashamed or afraid to get help. I got counseling, and I was on medication. You can recover and learn to love again. I believe that God has someone just for you.

Find a song that speaks to you and cling to it. The song that got me through was "Something Happens (Jesus)" by Bishop Paul S. Morton. I couldn't pray. I didn't feel that I could talk to anyone. No one seemed to understand how much pain I was in. I felt that some people just wanted me to get over it and move on. I would put that song on repeat play and peace would come over me. There's something about the name Jesus. There's power in the name Jesus. There's healing in the name Jesus. There's deliverance in the name Jesus.

I want to encourage women to stop settling just because you

don't want to be alone. Wait for God's best for you. You deserve it. Stop hurting other women. How would you feel if you were in the wife's shoes? Understand that some men will lie to get what they want. Don't believe everything they say. Find out for sure whether he is married or not. Most of all, don't give your body to anyone outside of marriage.

Young women, please do not allow older men to entice you into a relationship. Older men are attracted to younger women because you are more pliable than women their age. They can manipulate you into doing just about anything that satisfies their lust. They are giving you the attention and "love" that your absent or uninvolved father did not give you. Don't fall for the tricks. They only want personal gratification at your expense.

Let God love you. He will be your father. Then you will wait for the gentleman that you deserve. Today, I am healed, delivered, and set free by the grace of God. All glory to God!

THE MESSAGE

Please join me in saving marriages and families. There are too many children being raised in broken homes today because the divorce rate is so high. They are missing opportunities that they deserve to have. Please commit to not getting involved with someone whom you know is married or in a relationship. Get to know that person before getting into a serious relationship. And don't have sex outside of marriage. It may feel good right now, but sooner or later, it's going to bring you pain. Learn from my mistakes. Send that man back home to his wife. He can't do anything for you. If he can't honor his wedding vows with her, he won't honor them with you. If he can't stay committed to her, he won't stay committed to you. Marriage is about communication and commitment. Love is just one ingredient. Love is not all.

Sisters, let's unite to stop enabling men who have no self-control to cheat. If he were your husband, wouldn't you want her to say no? Yes, it will hurt her that he even approached you, and that needs to be addressed, but at least nothing physical happened. After the physical connection, emotions can develop, and then the situation is harder to handle; it's harder to walk away.

Whatever you put into the atmosphere will come back to you. For every person that you intentionally hurt, someone is going to hurt you. If he left her (his wife) for you, sooner or later, he's going to leave you for her (his next conquest). People usually don't change. If he's lying to you now, there will be more lies later. If he's cheating with you now, he will be cheating on you later. You are *not* special! You are *not* different! You are *not* better! He's lying to you. He's lying on her. What goes around, comes around. "For whatsoever a man soweth, that shall he also reap" (Gal. 6:7). Learn from my mistakes. Break the cycle. Stand for marriage.

Husbands, if there are problems in the bedroom, do something productive until you work it out. And do whatever it takes to work it out. Go to the gym and work out. Play basketball with the boys. Go for a run. You have to redirect that energy into a positive direction—a direction away from adultery. It's not all her fault. There's a problem, and you both need to get to the root of it, maybe even with a counselor. Stop taking the easy way out through a side chick. When your wife finds out about your affair and she is hurt, it's going to hurt you, too. The two of you are one, and what hurts her hurts you, too. Do the hard work, make your marriage work, and save your family. Most of all, put God first and keep him first in all things.

Also, the problem with preachers is that a lot of people put them on pedestals. People forget that pastors are human, that they are fallible, that they make mistakes just like we do. We lift them up and expect them to remain perfect. Then when they fall, we're quick to condemn them, to throw them under the bus. Yet, the higher we raise them on that pedestal, the easier it is for them fall off. We have to remember that they are human, too. The man in the pulpit recognizes a beautiful woman just like the man on the street does. And women should not be tempting these men. Recognize the man of God for who he is, and respect his position—and respect yourself. If great men like David, Samson, and Solomon can fall, certainly, men of today can, too.

Preachers, instead of feeding your lust with porn, you should be covering yourself with prayer. You have to die to self daily. Paul said, "I am crucified with Christ: nevertheless I live; yet not I, but Christ liveth in me: and the life which I now live in the flesh I live by the faith of the Son of God, who loved me, and gave himself for me" (Gal. 2:20). And he said, "For the good that I would I do not: but the evil which I would not, that I do. Now if I do that I would not, it is no more I that do it, but sin that dwelleth in me" (Rom. 7:19–20).

Pastors and preachers, take your commitment to God seriously. You promised to serve him and to shepherd his sheep. Do it in righteousness and in holiness. Gal. 6:8 tells us, "For he that soweth to his flesh shall of the flesh reap corruption; but he that soweth to the Spirit shall of the Spirit reap life everlasting." You are responsible for every soul in your flock and God *will* hold you accountable for hurting even one of his sheep. They are not to be used for your personal pleasure or your personal gain.

And we, as the body of Christ, must obey Gal. 6:1: "Brethren, if a man be overtaken in a fault, ye which are spiritual, restore such an one in the spirit of meekness; considering thyself, lest thou also be tempted."

Also, women should not be misled by anyone who calls himself a preacher. Just because he wears a robe or has a position of authority in the church does not mean that you follow him blindly. Do not allow him to manipulate you into sin. Use common sense; use spiritual sense. Try the Spirit by the Spirit. Sin is sin, whether it is committed by someone in a robe or not. The robe does not justify the sin, and it certainly does not cover the sin. Sex outside of marriage, no matter how he spins it, is wrong. Your body is a temple. Reverence it.

And, some women think being a first lady is glamorous and so easy, but it's not. It is a full-time job and a lot of hard work. They have to deal with not only the members' drama, but also the pastor's mess. He's human. He has flaws. He has emotions that are sometimes unchecked behind closed doors. He pours everything into the members, and sometimes he doesn't have anything left for his family. When the members drain him, the first lady has to pour back into him. Pastors need encouragement and prayer, too. They get discouraged and disappointed. They feel sadness and loss. Sometimes, they want to give up. There's a lot going on behind the scenes that we don't see. Pastors look really good out front, but go behind closed doors, and the view changes. A great first lady, however, makes it look easy. She makes it look glamorous. Blessings to all the great first ladies!

ROSALIND'S REVELATIONS

I can show you better than I can tell you. (Courtesy of Bea Baker.)

A man will change if he *chooses* to. You can *motivate* him to change, but you can't *make* him change.

They are broken, and *you* can't fix them. Only God can make them whole again.
#BoysPlayWithToysMenHandleTheirBusiness
#INeedMultipleWomenToValidateMyManhood
#CompensatingForMyDeficiencies

It's not that you're not woman enough; it's that he's not man enough.

Ladies, if you have to constantly fight to keep your man, you're with the wrong man. Let that fool go.
#YouDeserveBetterBeautifulWoman
#AQueenDeservesAKing

It's not your job to let other women know he's taken. It's his.

Lies, lies, lies.
Side chick, is he still your dream come true?
Or has he become your worst nightmare, too?

Instead of talking to your mistress about your wife, you should be talking to your wife about your mistress.

She's going to tell your wife. When you hurt her, when you make her mad, or when you don't give her what she wants— sooner or later, one way or another, your side chick is going to tell your wife.

The wife isn't always the last to know. Sometimes, she's one of the first to know.
#NotSoSubtleChanges
#NewHabits
#Something'sGoingOn
#IThinkMyHusbandIsCheatingOnMe

Your wife knows; she just isn't saying anything. She doesn't want to upset her life any more than it already is.

Men, think about your daughters. How would you feel if a man treated your daughter the way you treat women?

He may be a man of God, but he's a man, first.

Marriage is not about sex. Marriage is about love, commitment, and communication. Making love is the cherry on top.

If you don't love God, you can't love someone else.
#UnconditionalLove
#UnselfishLove
#EverlastingLove

Marriage is about commitment, not convenience. Marriage must be maintained.

Romance novels and soap operas are not blueprints for relationships and marriage.

Marrying someone is a whole new level from dating that person. In living with someone, you see everything twenty-four/seven. Your everything twenty-four/seven may not mesh with his everything twenty-four/seven. Can you stay committed in spite of the clash?

Through your public face, they only see your good. But behind closed doors, I see your good, your bad, and your ugly.

Let's have a *real* conversation *first*. What do you need? What do you want? What do you expect? In a relationship? In a marriage? From me?

Ask the hard questions before you get married. You won't be surprised and disappointed after you get married. "Man, she don't cook. She don't clean. She don't wanna have sex no more, but she wanna spend my money." "Girl, he want me to cook his dinner, clean his house, and open my legs whenever *he* gets ready."

It's best to talk about it now than fight about it later.

I, as a woman, need you to love on me before you make love to me.

Husband: "Baby, I know you need love and emotional support. I get that. And I love you with all my heart, but sometimes, I just want sex. It feels so good, and I need release to get relief."

Wives, if your husband enjoys attention from other women in public, maybe he's not getting what he needs from you in private. You might want to check yourselves. What you won't do, somebody else will.

Husbands, listen to your wives. They have "wifedar" that can detect a home-wrecker miles away, long *before* she gets up close and personal. If she has curves and she's always in your face about something, you better check yourselves. Her actions, even if her intentions happen to be pure, can influence your intentions and your actions in the wrong way. Her need of you is your Achilles heel. Protect yourself and listen to your wife.

Husbands, if another woman makes you feel the way your wife *used to* make you feel, don't lean into it. Step back and reevaluate your marriage. This is a sure sign that something is wrong.

If a man is not content with what he has at home, he is prone to drift away from home.

Don't get it twisted. When you introduce me, I am your best friend and your wife, Ros B. Just "my wife" depersonalizes me. Just "Ros B" removes the intimacy of our relationship.

When she (who is not your wife) has you backed into a corner, can you turn and walk away?

It's time to pull a Joseph. *Run!*

A woman needs to know that she is first in your life. If you put her first, she will allow you to put other things first from time to time.

How can I do this?
Because women are strong emotionally. We take what's thrown our way and we don't let it break us; we let it make us.

This struggle right now is not about me. It's about my destiny.
#StayOnThePath
#NoDetoursHere

Sisters, let's unite to stop enabling men who have no self-control to cheat. If he were your husband, wouldn't you want her to say no? Yes, it hurts that he even approached her, and that needs to be addressed, but at least nothing physical happened. After the physical connection, emotions can develop, and then the situation is harder to handle.

Let go of your plans for your life and grab hold of God's plans for your life. Then, you can move forward.

God will take little and make much.

Don't fight with fools; pray for them. Don't pray *about* them (God already knows); pray *for* them.

Petty people do not bother me. I understand that their actions come from a place of pain and/or insecurity.

Don't cut me down when I'm wrong. Build me up. There's a positive way to say something negative.
#CorrectionIsGood
#CorrectMeInLove

When people treat you badly and you feel like they're getting away with it: "God, why don't you *do* something?"
God says, "I am. I'm extending grace and mercy to them the same way I extend it to you."

Freewill
You can do it your way and suffer the consequences or you can do it God's way and reap the rewards.

STOP PRETENDING

It's time to stop pretending. People don't have power over you unless you give it to them. It doesn't matter what they think about you. It doesn't matter what they say about you. It doesn't matter what they try to do to you.

Years ago, people picked on you, bullied you, made you feel less than. You became an adult and said, "no more." You stood up to people. You became successful. You became an overachiever. People like you. They look up to you. You're the man. But- you have a secret. You're *not* all that. You're *not* altogether. You haven't arrived- really. It just looks that way. You're not as strong as you pretend to be- because you're hurting and the facade is starting to crumble. You're afraid. The cracks are showing. You can't pretend much longer.

You never dealt with the hurt, the ridicule, the rejection, the pain. You buried it, repressed it, denied it. But the roots are bursting through the surface. You can't contain them. You can't control them. It's all falling apart and you can't pretend any longer. People are starting to see your brokenness.

Stop pretending. You are broken but God is waiting to

mend you. He will help you. He will vindicate you. He will avenge you.

"He healeth the broken in heart, and bindeth up their wounds.

The LORD lifteth up the meek: he casteth the wicked down to the ground"

(Psa. 147:3, 6).

"Fear thou not; for I am with thee: be not dismayed; for I am thy God: I will strengthen thee; yea, I will help thee; yea, I will uphold thee with the right hand of my righteousness.

Behold, all they that were incensed against thee shall be ashamed and confounded: they shall be as nothing; and they that strive with thee shall perish" (Isa. 41:10-11).

CPSIA information can be obtained
at www.ICGtesting.com
Printed in the USA
BVHW050905140422
634330BV00006B/116